To Become Intimate With ME

LaTeka T. Mota

Table of Contents

PART 1

—

To Become Intimate with ME

Am I Running?

Am I running from YOU or MYSELF?
Is it good or bad for my HEALTH?
Don't need regret nor resentment.
AWWW here we go, might have to repent again.

Do you love me or not?
I cannot tell and my heart is hurting.
Gotta' heal from something else now.
When another healing is almost over,
YOU did something new now for me to heal from.

Should we continue to try or just leave?
I mean do you complete me?
As history is replayed in this present,
Your presence has not always been a blessing.

So tell me, AM I RUNNING?

An Increase

Water causes an increase
Love affects an increase
Supplication is an increase
We all demand an increase
In life there is an increase
In your mind there is an increase
In your body there is an increase
We all demand an increase
Within our spirit there is an increase
Religions give an increase
From knowledge there is an increase
We all need an increase
Using music gives me an increase
Applying the Word builds my increase
From literature and entertainment there's an increase
I have ways to increase

Appreciate YOU

Time is valued
Time is managed
Self-care is very significant
Loving yourself should be efficient
Let no one discourage what God has already encouraged
Be proud of YOURSELF
Put wealth back into your health
Remain kind and patient
Never afraid of elevation
Move forward
Embrace those challenges
Let those blessings descend
Have high faith to sustain any pain
Remember to meditate so you can maintain
Invite happiness into your life
No more strife
The world is hazardous
Access the damages
Stay true to you
Do what's best to progress

Attachment Issues

Issues, we all have them.
I am attached to you; are you attached to me?
Are we trying to fix these attachment issues?
Maybe so, maybe not.
I do still care.
My love for you will never just go away.
Being hopeful about us…
I want to regain trust.
You made me nervous initially,
Had me wondering could this really be.
You broke my heart.
We have attachment issues.
It can be mended with much attention and support.
I desired to be your wife.
Thought you were my potential husband.
With all these attachment issues,
Maybe we're better off without each other.

Bad Habits

Patterns of bad behavior

Still one with nature

How one copes with emotional and mental abuse

Can cause confusion

Don't lose yourself

Build your wealth

Dedicate and meditate

Don't let bad habits allow you to depreciate

When enough is enough

Rid your life of that habit

Realign… Shift… Accelerate

Bad habits create conflict

Depletion of them resolves it

Increase good over bad habits

For the greater good of your life to not be damaged

Comida: Food

Food is delicious.
Food is nutritious.
Food is diverse.
It is culturally authentic.
I love food.
It is good for my soul.
MI COMIDA; MY FOOD.
Oh how I love to cook.
So many recipes, now that's a cookbook.

Food for my tastebuds something spicy.
Not too sweet, not too salty.
Enrich my health inward and outward
Especially dark chocolate with its antioxidants

Food is designed to enjoy and relax with
To experiment, mix and blend make something unique
Oh how vegetables and fruits are good for me
MI COMIDA MY FOOD
Oh how I love to cook
So many recipes, now that's a cookbook.

Drama

I try to be drama free
It can still arrive no matter what
Preparation from readings and my churches gets me by
Drama can be random
Attack indirect or direct
Retract from it respectively
Isolate and replace with optimism
Refrain from pessimism
Let your light shine
No more drama allowed
No more drama around
I wish no drama could be found

Flaws

Within me there are several flaws
I am so guarded, It is hard to let down these walls
I can be a flower that blossoms
Or I can be a butterfly that flies away
To be complex yet submissive
Makes me worth the effort
My flaws are embraced
My flaws are forever changing
Some flaws are leaving or slowly decreasing
Although there is pain
My flaws adapt to the season
By committing to a plan
Seeking out desired goals
The flaws will continue to fall

Healthiness

Determination: I am determined to reach my destiny
Endless: Completeness will eventually come
Fulfillment: My glass is always half full
Intuition: My mind won't stop
New: I am refreshed daily
Love: I will always love this man
Protective: I protect my daughter at all costs
Protected: I can endure the natural with God's power
Beauty: Healthiness is reflected
Morals: This can be traditional
Rules: There are stipulations
The outcome is healthiness

History

We didn't make it to the future,
now you are a part of my HISTORY.
I thought I would never lose you,
your love was a mystery.
Your behavior changed too quickly,
and not for the best.
The relationship has ended,
I suppose You were a test.

We are HISTORY. Oh yes indeed,
I wonder, my mind did you ever feed.
HISTORY in the making, I'll say that too,
there was no love; there is no proof.
Pain instead of pleasure to gain—
We are a part of each other's HISTORY,
and that will remain.

Identity

I am serious about who I am
My appearance does not define me
My heart loves to love
I have been used before
It may have happened again
However, God created me for a reason
Our relationship will never die
Joyful cries equal a balanced tomorrow
He is the reason why
Identity begins not at birth, but from God inside
     the womb
God prepares me, gives me room
My identity is special
Just like everyone else
Our identity constantly develops and manifests
Into who He wants and needs us to be
We should embrace our God-given identity.

In the Moment

A hallelujah shouted unto You
From all your people here on earth
Who need to hear a word or two
The Bible comes in many translations
So we can always receive a revelation
And brings us back to salvation
No good deed ever ignored in your book
When God rises the devil better be shook
He a copycat but You be the original authenticator
The awesome creator my musical instrument
I stay equip full of godly resources
They quench my thirst
We better put God first
Let the past be the past, bygones be bygones
You know you strong
With God He'll carry you, help you hold on
Don't descend ascend
From beginning to the end
Now, can I get an "amen"?

Rescue

An overflow of sorrow
Do not know which way to go
Gotta RESCUE myself
To make room to grow
I am high when I fly
Soaring to the sky
Gotta RESCUE myself
Do not have downtime

I share and I care
Without love do I dare
Gotta RESCUE myself
Only time will tell
The definition of love is infinite
I am glad God continues to give it
My Lord and Savior helped produce
My little Miracle

Kind Eyes

Eyes are enchanting
Eyes can be deceiving
Though eyes can be kind
We have to mind our eyes
Eyes are glossy and embracing
Makes mental notes of memories amazing
You are still one of a kind with your kind eyes and all
However the high has begun to fall
Although I may need you
I love myself more
Now this relationship has become a bore
Your kind eyes do not mean what they say
Therefore why should we stay?
Kind eyes can get you in trouble
To love or not to love
Is the question I ask

Life

Obstacles come and go
The pain I try not to show
Life can be difficult yet rewarding
More information learned more discovery earned
I try not to stress not to fret
More problems may arise once I forget or regret
Joyful moments, equal easy days
Bad memories equal tears
Laughter brings excitement
Music is for me to enjoy
Without my peaceful resources
I would not be able to do the most
Remain productive, focused and balanced
So, life may hit you hard
May cause a shift or a decline
Eventually, your life will redesign

Loved

I am loved

I am me

I am Cinderella Da Queen

I am LTM

I am talented

I am gifted

I am an excellent cook

I am poetic

I am goofy

I am moody

I am a fighter

I am systematic

I am spontaneous, too

I am confident

I am an outcast

I am loved

LTM

L is for Learning
A is for Attractive
T is for Thoroughbred
E is for Energized
K is for Keen
A is for Attentive

T is for Tedious
A is for About Love
M is for Miracle Baby
I is for Introvert
A is for Accountable

M is for Misunderstood
O is for Occupied
T is for Trying my Best
A is for A Changing Mood

More

More Trust
More Communication
More Adventure
More of YOU

More Quality Time
More Dates
More Playfulness
More of YOU

More Love
More Respect
More Drive
More of YOU

More Energy
More Aggression
More Affection
More of YOU

Myself

Jovial, Playful This I am
I desire happiness for others
I am content MYSELF
Satisfied by simple things
It can be the little things that count
Love, honesty and respect are very important to me
My daughter symbolizes a part of MYSELF
She represents my better self
I am proud of myself for not stopping
I have to watch my daughter grow up
I play a factor in our relationship
I finally invested in MYSELF

No Games

Don't play games I need you to be real
Express those emotions, tell me how you feel
Open up, talk a bit more
No games needed, I am on your side
Always ready to ride to have fun with you
Dates, pillow fights, dancing is nice
We can always be each other's spice
No mind games, only good ones allowed
I want that high back from you that I had once found
We do not need to play 'no games
We should fight for each other
No games, just love

Pressured

Did we pressure each other too much?
Did we not pressure each other enough?
My love is real, there's no pressure there
But are you truly genuine with your care?
Pressured to succeed
Pressured to become the best me
Pressured to compromise
Pressured to gain wisdom, to remain wise
I want to continue to be pressured
Because it is motivating my mind

Eventually to feel pressure will not exist
Although to be pressured is hard to resist

Relationships

Relationships go beyond our imagination
With God there is a beautiful creation
I've found love and in him there is trust
He holds my heart in his hands because I know I have
 a good man
I am his woman for life and without him there is strife
He is the one that God has sent from above

We will soon be married, until death do us part
To the most ambitious, courageous man of them all
I am there to catch him when he falls
Us together is worth more than a wedding ring
I give him me to have and to hold
Cherish every single day
Thank you, JESUS
For I would not have it any other way

Release Me

Take me away somewhere I've never been before
Let me soar, let me fly with you
Let me be everything I can to you
Release me
Relieve me of my pain that I still have
Take control and never let go
I'm in your heart
I know you care because you say so
You act like my man
You are my man
When can we see each other again?
Release me
I love you and I told you last night
You replied, "I can't wait to fall in love with 'T.'"
My poetry and songs are how we connect,
So through respect and dedication our love will always
    be amazing
Release me
Spiritually, mentally physically and emotionally
You have Teka T.

Religions

Religions are the continents to my spiritual globe
My spirit remains covered by GOD first
My spirituality is connected
Muslima Christiana
A hint of Buddhism
That's the mantra in me
I call that meditation sleep
Religions are the continents to my spiritual globe
His blood
That rainwater
From my head to my toes

Self-Sufficient

I am independent. God made me.
My mom taught me to be self-sufficient.
I am respectful.
I am generosa.
My mother raised me to be strong.
I must stay self-sufficient.
I am capable to love the right man.
I love to see others laughing.

I am high off GOD.
All of his resources help me rebuke the devil.
I will always be self-sufficient.

Sins

The act of a sin
Equals trouble
The consequence of a sin
Equals pain
We must reduce sinning to continue winning
No more sins means no more losses
When I try not to sin I gain
If I do not sin, I stay in my Godly place
Seek and I will find
God protects me every time
The act of a sin prolongs my blessings
Committing a sin places me in the wrong direction
But God and Jesus is my progression
To keep me in succession

Sixteen

Trauma began
Now it is deeper
I lost you
There was a lot of grieving
Calling on my first father
Crying very loudly
Even then I felt him surround me
I never doubted God
Even though I could not comprehend
He will always be my first best friend
Sixteen was crucial
Some pain is still there
I leaned on you to hold my hand
My eyes withhold so many stories
Some come with abuse
Aggression has built
Hostility too
Memories from sixteen are a part of my truth

Trying

Relationships: love and trust
I AM TRYING
Open-mindedness and compromise
I AM TRYING
Aware, alert and Attentive
I AM TRYING
Completely satisfied
I AM TRYING
Loving you unconditionally
I AM TRYING
Readily available
I AM TRYING
Committed to you
NOW THAT I AM ALWAYS
FAITHFUL AND HONEST
NOW THAT I AM ALWAYS TRYING

What I'm Learning

Learning new things is challenging
2005 was my new beginning
I love my spiritual bliss
One has to live each day to the fullest
I have so many dreams and expectations
My mind expands beyond imagination
My personality consists of creation
Each person deserves a celebration

The Sky is the limit
Whatever we need just PRAY
LOVE LIVE LIFE is one of my mottos
Everyone in their own way is adorable

Within Him

Compassion, affection all in one direction
Love is such an incredible, unimaginable, sensational
    feeling
He has changed by showing me all of what love really
    means
Laughter among other things is what joy brings
His eyes are so intense that I feel immense in the love
    he gives
Passion and faithfulness are building this heavenly bliss
It's like paradise, he's real and I love
I am so blessed for what God has given
He is the best not like any other
Within him true love has been discovered
I think, no I know, he's my soulmate
For my heart is filled with more pleasure than pain
There's much more to gain
He's like my secondary foundation of a new relation
With an outstanding beginning and an everlasting
    ending
Constantly showing me the light to happiness
The intensity within a conversation
For he is such an inspiration

PART 2

——

Spirituality: The Spirit In Me

A Forever Glow

When I shine it is because of you.
No man will or can take the place of my God.
You fulfill me by fulfilling my life.
When you gave me my daughter, she gave me a reason
    to live.
I owe myself to you.
You are my forever glow.

Your light so strong I must hold on.
You always reveal when it is time.
That is why I feel you working on the inside.
A forever glow I will forever know.
Forever I shall grow.

A Natural High

Our omnipresent Father
A natural high
His unconditional love
A natural high
Being so forgiving
A blessing
Sacrificing for the people
A blessing
Removing anything that is not of him
A supernatural high
Turning the pain into a blessing
Allowing us to learn from our lessons
Being the best provider and hero
Because of who you are and all you continue to do in
      your people's lives is what I call…a natural high

A Powerful Father

G is for generous
O is for omnipresent
D is for divine

You are a powerful father

G is for glorified
O is for opportunities
D is for demands attention

You are a powerful Father

G is for goal-oriented
O is for outstanding
D is for determined

You are a powerful Father

Blessings

Blessings are beautiful
And are given by the most generous one
Lessons come from blessings
They are very much earned

Blessings can be in the form of a miracle
And sometimes supernatural
Joy comes from blessings
It is reaped from sowing

Blessings are significant
And are effective to the abundance in people
Answers come from blessings
For problems are handled

Blessings.. blessings.. blessings
We all love to be blessed

Blessings

His blood covers us all
His blood saved us all
We're always covered by the almighty
Our sins are covered
Our health is covered
Being covered means we have a shield
The love keeps us covered
I try my best to stay covered
Doing my part doing the work
God helps me first
Being covered means we're special to Him
The creator meant to create
He is sweet
This is serious business
His voice is heaven sent
I am glad for my child-like playful ways
He keeps me covered
Ready for any day

Day of Rest

S is for savior
A is for arrived
B is for blessed
B is for bridging together
A is for attention-seeker
T is for timely
H is for healing

D is for delightful
A is for accustomed
Y is for youth

Describing God

Endurance, growth, guidance
All three of these, God supplies it
No weapon formed can prosper
That is why He is our number one Father
He loves us unconditionally
We shall never deny Him
God ignites and illuminates the fire inside us
He sits in the sky
And watches us with His peaceful eyes
That freeness, peacefulness
Yeah, it comes from Jesus
He is the reason for all the seasons
The mercy and grace can never be erased
For his love for us is captivating,
ELEVATING, REMARKABLE
AND OFFERS MANY SPARKLES
OF LITTLE AND BIG MIRACLES
IN OUR LIVES
FROM SUNRISE TO SUNSET
ALWAYS SHOW GOD RESPECT

Dreams

Dare
Reach
Every
Almighty
Miracle

Drive
Respect
Every
Action
Made
Supernaturally

Dive
Returning
Every
Act
Moved
Sophisticated
Dreams

For the Parents

Parents love their children with all their hearts
It's hard to let go when a child has to part
Safety and protection is a must
A parent must always have trust
To a mother, giving birth is a miracle
And raising a child is spiritual
To a father, having a son or daughter makes him happy
Just to hear those words "I love you daddy…"
Children are angels through our parent's eyes
When we are mischievous it's a surprise
Even though a child may make mistakes,
The love a parent has could never be erased
No matter what a child does,
Our parents will always be there for us
A parent has aspirations and expectations for their child
When we achieve, they smile

Free

God resolved
I received
God made me remember
All the beautiful things
Therefore, I remain free

God continues to heal me
I am constantly replenishing
God made me remember
All the beautiful things
My memories are free

God keeps me free
I am free
So, keep my mind on thee

Happy News

Jesus makes us feel good
This is always happy news
Eternal joy comes from them
Without God nothing is possible whatsoever

I love me some Jesus
He is the best bruh bruh
My Father is my first husband and best friend
He is with me until the very end
Love, wholesomeness, protection, and healing is given
    at any time
Grace, understanding, and attention is there all the time

Great discipleship is rewarded in private and in public
Obedience is a must to receive the most

Mi Hija: My Daughter

My daughter is my best friend under God
My daughter is well taken care of
My daughter is intelligent
My daughter is well-behaved
She is a fast learner
An enthusiastic reader
A joyful spirit to be around
An excellent dancer
Excited about school
A great athlete
My daughter is my only child
SHE MADE ME BECOME A BETTER WOMAN
My daughter is a success
She is an achiever

My Main Help

Throughout troubled times,
For me to go the distance
Fight that struggle
I know God is my main help
When I'm unsure of which path to take
When my body needs to refill
If I feel uneasy
Jesus is my main help
To become greater
To become stronger
To one day be completely healed
I know both are my main help
Not another can be God
Not another can be Jesus
Not another can touch me the way they do
No one else can ever be my main help
Hallelujah
Amen

Peace of Mind

You give me light that shines so brightly
You give me hope to continue to go on with my life
You give me courage to be what I know I can
You give me peace of mind
Because of your newness and greatness
You are a wonderful God with so much to offer
Your amazing grace is remarkable
Your love is beautiful
When I talk to you, I see heaven
Good vibes knowing you are around all the time
For that equals paradise
I love you so much
You give me peace of mind
I need you always
God you are faithful and good to me
I promise to remain true faithful and real to my Lord
My faith remains restored
Happiness and love is what you show me
Righteousness on a godly journey
I stay trying to seek

Pillowy Cloud

When I wanna' sail away
Escape to another form of paradise
I ask for my pillowy cloud
When I'm daydreaming of heavenly memories
Or need a time out
I ask for my pillowy cloud
Becoming one within myself
Conversing with you
Climbing to the mountains
I ask for my pillowy cloud
The way you take care of me
The way you console me
The way you fulfill
I will always ask for my pillowy cloud

Simplistic

He is simply simplistic
He is oh so sweet
He gives us choice without being controlling
He gives us will power to keep on rolling
He is generous without a doubt
He pulls me in through His Word
He generates my fight
Gives me might
He is simply simplistic
He is not hard to find
Just invite the Lord in
From Messiah to the Father
Don't forget the Holy Spirit
He is simply simplistic

Spirituality

S is for soul
P is for Prayers
I is for Inviting
R is for Rituals
I is for Invigorating
T is for Truthful
U is for Unique
A is for Atonement
L is for Long lasting
I is for Inner peace
T is for Totally rewarding
Y is for Yes factor

That Light

My God, his light shines so vividly
He is such imagery
I can testify
For the many things He has let me see
Jesus is His Son
He was chosen
There is a calling and a mission
I'm thankful to be forgiven
That light
I need it, want to feel
How it touches my soul like my food
He is oh so real
That light stay bright
I see right

What Consists of Love

Love is life and life is love
but what happens in-between is oh so rough
Instead of happiness, there is pain
However, in the end there will be pleasure to gain
With respect and dedication there needs to be patience
Honor one another like one does thy father and mother
Satisfy your mate and cherish the life together
Be able to compromise to make it through any type
    of weather
The soul needs to be replenished before our lives
    are ended
Mixing love with sin is dangerous
To maintain just be faithful
No one is perfect just make it work
Husbands and wives are in for a big surprise
What feels right might not be so tight
Life is beyond our imagination and love is exhilarating
    but to comprehend and
compromise one must be wise
Be there to sympathize and wipe away the tears from
    his or her eyes

The Present

Crying releases my pain
But the pain won't go away
Frustration and complication is part of the situation
I use meditation instead of medication
I have much determination for replacing and restoring
My faith in me
I can succeed no I will succeed
Learning how to make sacrifices
To sustain my peace
I've been to hell and back
And that is a fact
That's why I feel so blessed
Even though there's a storm within my cloud
I have been found
Placed in the direction of the light
The ultimate paradise
God is always with me
And He has forgiven thee

Author Bio

Nature and God's green scenery intrigues me mentally. Muslima Christiana with a hint of Buddhism is the religion that is the globe to my spiritual continents. Then, my daughter and friends encourage me to be a better version of myself at all times. Music and literature are a constant reminder to inspire the success path, along with furthering my education. My fight is so strong that my faith in myself and GOD keeps me persevering.

One must not ever give up on thyself. This poetry references my lifestyle on relational and spiritual levels. I want everyone to be happy, love themselves, and find a significant other to cherish life with. It is truly a reflection of me, LaTeka Tamia Mota.

Connect and Share

If you enjoyed this book of poems, please purchase copies for your friends and family and leave a review online at Amazon.com.

Connect with the author at
https://m.facebook.com/dominicanadiva7
https://instagram.com/brooklynmolta
https://twitter.com/dominicanadiva7
E-mail: motalateka@gmail.com

www.ingramcontent.com/pod-product-compliance
Lightning Source LLC
Chambersburg PA
CBHW070944120626
46546CB00004B/1548